This book belongs to

Property is Theft!

The Corbyn Colouring Book

James Nunn

First published in the United Kingdom by Old Street Publishing 2015

ISBN 978-1-901400-395

A catalogue record for this book is available from the British Library.

Printed and bound in Great Britain by
TJ International Ltd, Padstow, Cornwall

The Corbyn Colouring Book

James Nunn

after an idea by *Oli Munson*

For Marmite (and Treacle, wherever he is).

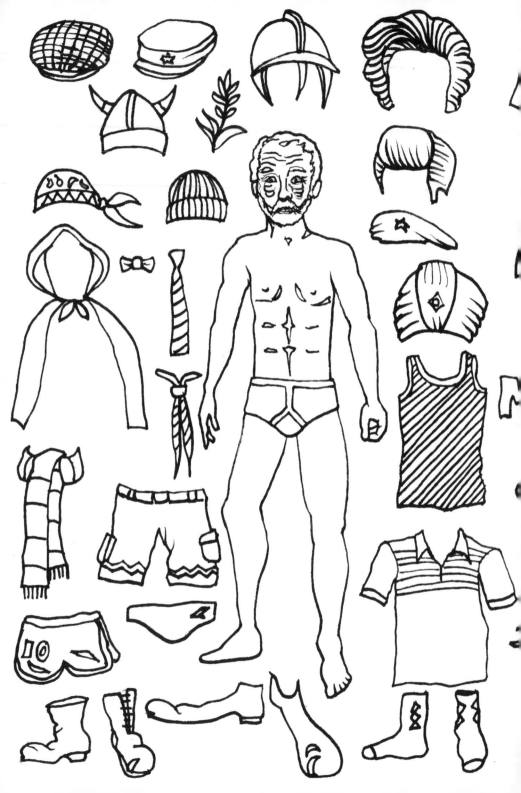

Left-Wing Beards

Draw your Own
Left-Wing Beards

Coalition Tongue Twister

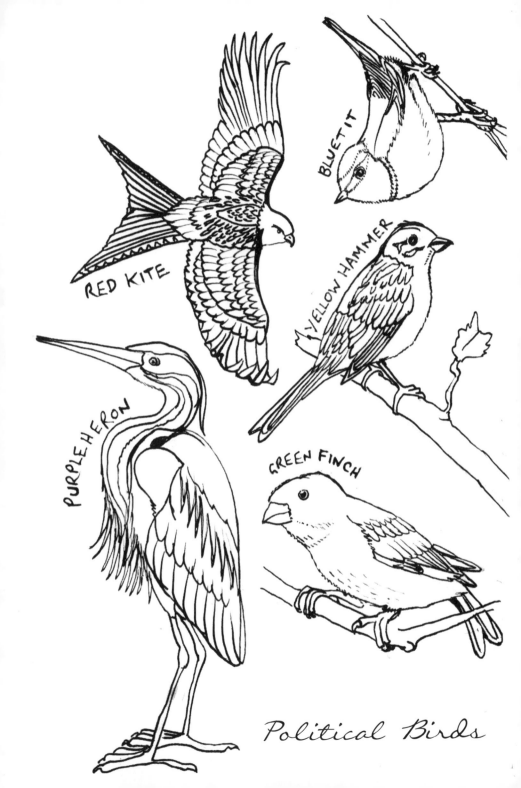

BLUE TIT

RED KITE

YELLOW HAMMER

PURPLE HERON

GREEN FINCH

Political Birds

Who's in Engels' Beard?

Colour Your
Borough

Find the subliminal message in Jeremy's beard...

Watch out for subliminal messages in Jeremy's beard

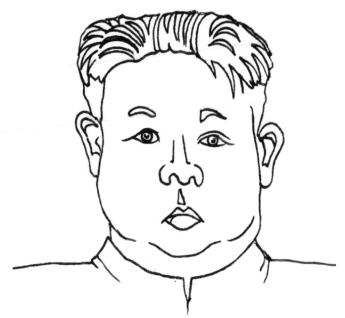

Dangerous Beardless Lefties
(and Tony Blair)

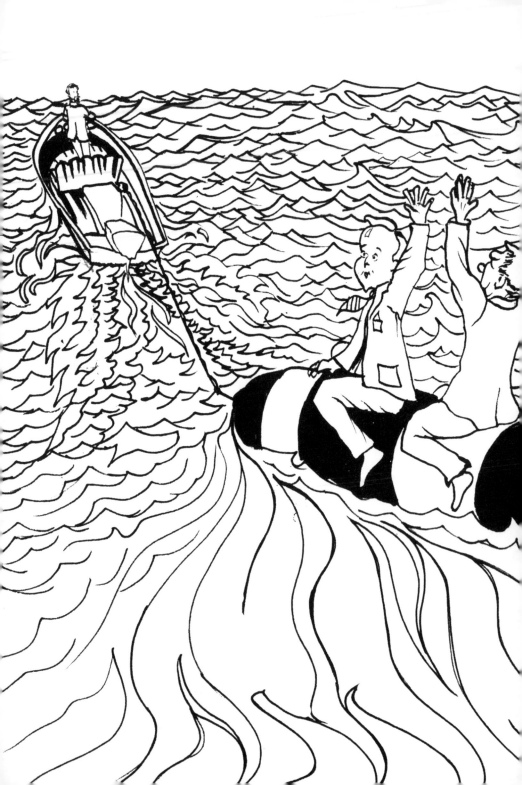

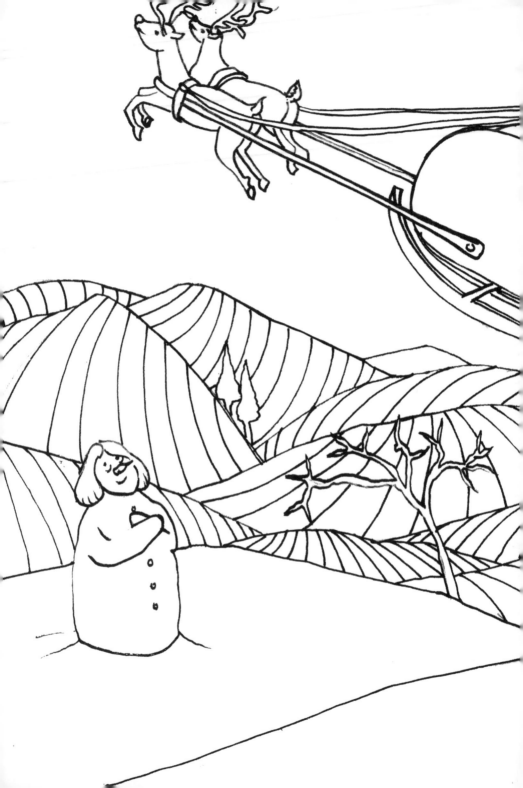

Acknowledgements

It has been my dream since before I can remember (but after the point at which I was able to dream) to draw silly pictures of renegade lefties who have greatness thrust upon them. Sincere thanks must go to my extraordinary publisher, Ben Yarde-Buller, for making this possible and for pushing me to do better when my drawings of our dough-faced premier did not come up to scratch. I would also like to thank all the friends and colleagues who came up with ideas for the drawings. Special mention must go to Zoe Macdonald who gets all the cigars for the *Beardless Lefties* and *Bynman* and several other moments of clarity that proved to be priceless contributions. Thank you to Tim Armstrong who introduced me to Proudhon and of course to Mr Corbyn for providing his beautiful, sad, lived-in face, and for kicking against the pricks. Finally, thanks to Kathleen, Sam, George, Elizabeth, Mum and Caroline, who have been putting up with this sort of nonsense for far too long. You make me the idiot I am and I thank you.

James Nunn
Bath, 2015